START-A-CRAFT

Batik

START-A-CRAFT

Batik

Get started in a new craft with easy-to-follow

projects for beginners

JOY CAMPBELL

CHARTWELL
BOOKS, INC.

A QUINTET BOOK

Published by Chartwell Books
A Division of Book Sales, Inc.
110 Enterprise Avenue
Secaucus, New Jersey 07094

This edition produced for sale in the U.S.A.,
its territories and dependencies only.

ISBN 0-7858-0063-8

This book was designed and produced by
Quintet Publishing Limited
6 Blundell Street
London N7 9BH

Creative Director: Richard Dewing
Designer: James Lawrence
Project Editor: Katie Preston
Editor: Lydia Darbyshire
Photographers: Paul Forrester
and Laura Wickenden

Typeset in Great Britain by
Central Southern Typesetters, Eastbourne
Manufactured in Hong Kong by
Regent Publishing Services Limited
Printed in China

ACKNOWLEDGMENTS

The Publisher would like to thank
George Weil and Candlemakers for supplying
equipment for photography.

The batik on p48 (top left) was kindly loaned
by Josie Cowan.

The batik on p2 is from the Kelik Gallery,
Yogyakarta, Java.

DEDICATION

For Kieran and Joseph

Contents

INTRODUCTION

———— ◇ ————

Batik is an ancient method of applying colored designs to fabric. It is called a "resist" method because traditionally hot wax is used to penetrate the cloth to prevent or "resist" the dye from spreading to areas so protected. Rice paste or mud is sometimes used instead of wax. Designs may be of one color or many, depending on the number of times the resists are applied and the fabric is dipped into baths of different dyes. Modern, simple-to-use dyes mean the technique of "pool" batik can be used. In this process wax is applied to surround complete areas of fabric and to prevent the dye from spreading from one area to another, which means that colors used next to each other give results that would be more difficult to achieve by the traditional immersion method.

The precise origins of batik are disputed. There is early evidence of batik in the form of garments depicted in Indian wall paintings; linen cloth dating to the 5th century has been excavated in Egypt; in Japan batik was made into silk screens from the 8th century, the work probably being carried out by Chinese artists; and in Java 13th-century temples show figures possibly wearing batik cloth. It is more certain that as early as A.D. 581 batik was being produced in China and probably being exported to Japan, central Asia, the Middle East, and India via the Silk Route.

Wherever it originated, however, the batik method was adopted more enthusiastically in Indonesia, especially Java, than anywhere else. It was the Javanese who developed the canting (pronounced "chanting" and originally spelled *tjanting*) to facilitate and refine the application of wax. It is basically a metal bowl to hold the hot wax, with a spout through which the wax is poured, and a wooden handle. The invention of the canting opened up the possibility of producing the wonderfully intricate array of designs seen particularly in Javanese batiks.

The word "batik" derives from the Javanese word, *tik*, meaning spots or dots. Early batiks were executed by means of tiny dots of wax, which were applied to the fabric to form the design. By the 13th century it had become a highly developed art, a fitting leisure pastime for women of noble birth. They often took months to complete a piece of fabric, just as an aristocratic European lady might have stitched her fine needlework.

Early batik designs were believed to have magical powers which would protect the person who wore them, and individual designs were reserved for particular noble families. The Garuda symbol, which was associated with prosperity and success in life, for example, could be used only by members of the royal courts. Today, this creature, half-man, half-eagle, who carried the god Vishnu, has become the national symbol of Indonesia, just as batik fabric has become the national dress of Java.

The production of batik fabric became the main industry and export of Java, from which it spread throughout the world. It was brought to Europe via Holland after the colonization of Java by the Dutch in the early 17th century. By the 1830s several factories had been established in Europe, and these used Indonesian techniques, taught by Indonesians, who were brought to Holland specifically for that purpose.

By the 1840s the Javanese were using caps (pronounced "chops" and originally spelled *tjaps*), a form of block to print the wax on with. These were adapted from an Indian technique, and they made the process faster, an advance that made the production of imitation batik sarongs in Switzerland uneconomical.

A group of Eurasian women, called collectively the Indische School of Batik, produced fabric for Dutch colonial officials and their families. Their designs, which were a combination of the traditional, intricate forms of Java and the color and simplicity of China, became very fashionable in the early years of the 20th century. Also around the late 1800s, the British African print trade began, and more styles were incorporated into batik fabric designs. Africans had produced resist-dyed fabrics for centuries — the Yoruba of western Africa used cassava paste as a resist, while the

people of Senegal used rice paste. In India, where cotton was used instead of silk, the batik industry reached its zenith in the 17th and 18th centuries.

Western production of batik on a large scale collapsed with the general economic decline after World War I, and the skill reverted to being the domain of the individual craftsman in Indonesia. In Europe artists and craftsmen continued to work in batik, developing and experimenting with its possibilities. In the 1920s modern dyestuffs started to replace traditional vegetable dyes, changing the appearance of batik fabric by bringing deeper, darker, and more varied shades to the range of possible colors.

Batik is undergoing a revival in appreciation and interest in the West. In addition to the traditional uses of batik fabric for clothes and soft furnishings, the medium's potential is being explored and applied as a fine art, with artists seeking expression through dye instead of paint. However, it is still to Indonesia, especially to Java, that the batik enthusiast goes to learn firsthand about the process and the art.

BELOW Traditional batiked material from Indonesia.

EQUIPMENT AND MATERIALS

In the projects described in this book, you will gradually gain the knowledge you need to accomplish a wide variety of batik pieces. The basic methods, equipment, and materials you will need are discussed in the projects, and I have introduced new techniques in this gradual way so that newcomers to the craft are not overwhelmed and discouraged before they have even begun. You do not need to be able to draw in the first few projects, and motifs are printed for your use where necessary until you gain confidence to find or make up your own. All of the projects do, however, use a number of basic pieces of equipment and materials, and I have listed these below, together with the quantities you will need. The only exception is the first project, the greeting cards, for which you need only the first 11 items.

You will need

◊ Plastic sheet to protect your work surface. Large plastic bags can be cut open and used. Choose white rather than black so that you can see any dye.

◊ Cotton balls.

◊ Sponge, 1in thick by 12in square.

◊ Rubber gloves – thin surgical-weight ones are best.

◊ Iron – preferably use an old one in case you get wax on it.

◊ Newspaper.

◊ Measuring spoons. You will need to be able to measure 1 tablespoon, 1 teaspoon, ½ teaspoon, and ¼ teaspoon.

◊ Dyes – 1oz of MX 8G (yellow), MX G (turquoise), MX G (blue), MX 5B (cerise), and MX CWNA (Procion black). These are all Procion fiber-reactive dyes.

◊ 2-cup measuring cup.

◊ 1lb sodium carbonate (washing soda) or soda ash.

◊ 1lb sodium bicarbonate (baking soda).

◊ 1lb urea – this is obtainable from specialist suppliers.

◊ 2lb batik wax – this quantity should be enough for all of the projects, although you could start off with a 1lb packet. This is available from specialist suppliers.

◊ Wax pot – some cheaper alternatives are discussed on page 14, but if you are going to do a lot of batik, you should buy a wax pot from a specialist. I have used a wax pot set on mark 5 for all the projects in this book.

◊ Natural bristle brushes, small and medium sizes and both flat and round for making different marks.

◊ Cantings – small, medium, and large spouts should be sufficient, with perhaps one novelty multispout. Indonesian cantings are the best if you can get them.

◊ Soft, absorbent cloths (rags will do).

◊ Scouring kit – a large saucepan, detergent, and wooden tongs (see page 16).

◊ Fabric – 6yd of 36-in wide lightweight cotton should be ample for all the projects in the book and allow for some mistakes, too. It must be 100 percent cotton, not polycotton. You will also need 1yd silk, although 18in would be sufficient. All fabric has to be prepared – that is, scoured and ironed – before you start a piece of work. If you buy 6yd cotton and want to scour it all at once, you can put it into the hottest wash in your machine with half your normal amount of ordinary detergent, although this will vary according to the softness of your water. Do **not** boil silk.

LEFT A wax pot, caps, cantings, and wax brushes.

BELOW The five basic dye colors you will need.

Chemicals, dyes, and hot wax should all be treated with respect. Follow the safety tips throughout the book, and you will have fun and peace of mind.

SAFETY FIRST

● Do not inhale the fine dye powder, and if it comes in contact with your eyes, rinse them immediately in plenty of clean water.

GREETING CARDS

◇

The simplest kind of batik you can do is on paper using ordinary white
household candles to apply the wax resist. You can use almost any kind of paper
as long as it is not coated with a shiny finish and is not too flimsy — photocopying
paper is usually suitable. Making these greeting cards introduces you to working
with the soda solutions, mixing and applying dyes, ironing out, and seeing the
"halo" that results from wax seeping when you iron your work.

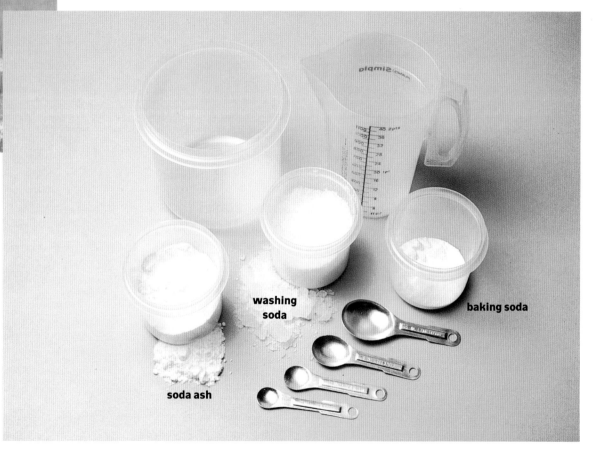

You will need
- ◊ Basic equipment, first 11 items
- ◊ Sheets of white paper, 8 × 10in
- ◊ Hairdryer (optional)
- ◊ Two or three white household candles
- ◊ Cardboard to make a viewing window (use an empty cereal box)
- ◊ Ready-made, cutout window cards to mount your finished work
- ◊ Stick glue or spray adhesive

1 So that the dye penetrates the paper
properly, you should prepare it with a solution
of 1 teaspoon baking soda and 1 teaspoon
washing soda dissolved in 1½ pints of warm
water. You can use soda ash instead of
washing soda, but it is twice as strong so you
need add only ½ teaspoon to the water. If it is
kept in an airtight container, this solution
remains usable for 10–14 days.

2 Lay a sheet of paper on a flat, non-
absorbent surface, such as formica or glass.
Use cotton balls to apply the soda solution
evenly over the paper. Soak the paper
thoroughly, but do not rub it so hard that you
begin to roughen the surface. Leave the paper
to dry completely; wax will not penetrate
where there is water. If you want to speed up
the drying time, use a hairdryer, or iron the
paper between sheets of newspaper with the
iron set to low. Ironing may cause the paper to
crinkle, but this often adds interesting effects.
You could try it both ways — smooth and
wrinkled.

3

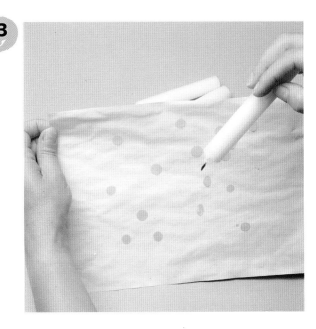

4

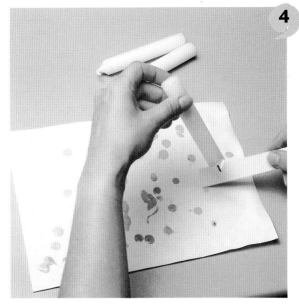

5

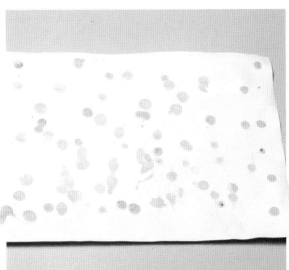

6

7

8

3 Place your prepared sheet of paper on the work surface. Light a candle and, as the wax melts, let it drip onto the paper. Experiment, holding it 3 inches above the paper, then 12 inches above the paper. Tip the paper at an angle, and move the candle quickly across the sheet.

4 Use a piece of cardboard to push the molten wax around the paper.

5 Notice the changes in the tone and degree of transparency of the paper as the hot wax cools.

6 Cover your work surface with a plastic sheet to protect it from the dye. Mix ¼ teaspoon yellow dye powder to a paste with a few drops of the soda solution. Add 2 tablespoons soda solution to this paste. The dye is ready to use. If you want a paler color, dilute the dye powder still further.

7 Use a large brush or a piece of cut sponge to color two stripes of yellow on your waxed paper. Wear rubber gloves when you do this, or your fingers will turn yellow, too.

8 Mix blue or turquoise dye powder in the same way and paint or sponge on two blue stripes. Leave it to dry completely. You can speed this up with a hairdryer, but don't hold it so close that you melt the wax.

SAFETY FIRST

● Good ventilation is important at all times, but especially when you are ironing wax. Work with your iron on one side so that your face is not directly above it. You may even wish to wear a mask as protection against the wax fumes released by the heat of the iron.

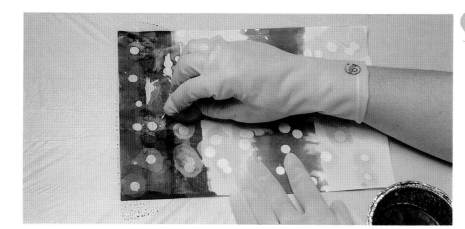

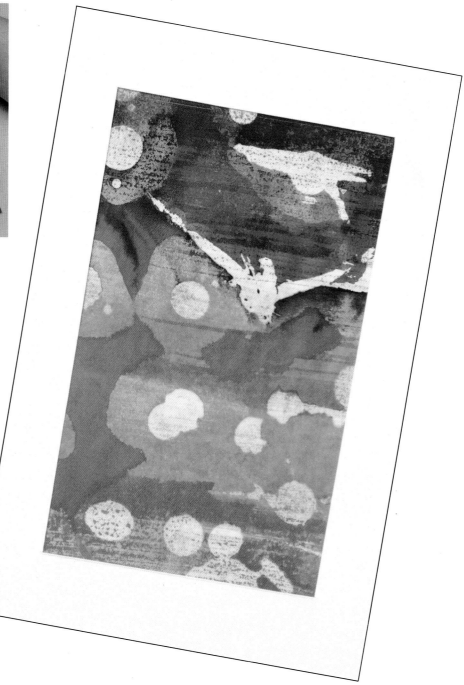

9 The wax is removed by ironing out between sheets of newspaper. Always make sure that there is a thick layer of newspaper under your batik to protect the surface below. Place two sheets of newspaper on top and use the iron on the cotton setting. You will see the wax melting and being absorbed into the newspaper. Continue to iron, putting fresh sheets of newspaper above and below your work, until no more wax comes out.

10 When the wax is ironed out, it also spreads into the paper around the original waxed areas, creating a "halo" effect. These "halo" areas will now also resist the dye, leaving abstract, unwaxed shapes, which can be dyed a third color if you wish.

11 When the dye has dried completely, use a viewing window to select areas, and you will have three or four "alien landscape" cards to send to your friends.

GIFT WRAP

———— ◇ ————

How about making some exclusive wrapping paper for a special present or a waterproof jacket for a precious book? You can melt some ordinary candles or use ready-made batik wax, which comes in the form of granules and is a mixture of paraffin (candle) wax and beeswax. Paraffin wax is brittle, cracks easily, and sometimes flakes off. Beeswax is soft and pliable when it is cool and adheres well to fabrics. The combination of the two balances their properties so that the wax will crack to give the traditional batik effect when it is folded but not so much that it flakes off. The ratio is about 70 percent paraffin to 30 percent beeswax. This project involves using a soft bed, mixing colors, and applying extra wax to remove "halos." It also introduces you to using caps.

You will need
◊ Basic equipment, plus
◊ Sheets of soda-treated paper,
  11 × 16 ins
◊ Small blanket or towel

Cap-making kit
◊ Masking tape
◊ Scissors/mat knife
◊ Empty cereal boxes
◊ Boxes
◊ Corrugated cardboard
◊ Cardboard tubes
◊ Corks

1

2

1 Whichever kind of wax you decide to use, you will need a way of melting it and keeping it hot. The safest, most reliable equipment is one of the thermostatically controlled, electric wax pots that are available from specialist suppliers. Here, the batik wax granules are beginning to melt.

2 To apply the wax, make some homemade versions of Indonesian caps, the copper printing blocks developed by the Javanese to print repeat patterns on lengths of fabric and so speed up the process of batik. Your caps can be made from cardboard rolls or from cut and folded cardboard, held with masking tape if necessary. Cutting with pinking shears gives an interesting tool, and corrugated cardboard is a good material to use because the loops serve as a reservoir for the wax. You could also use corks or wooden spools, but do not use any form of plastic, which will melt in the hot wax.

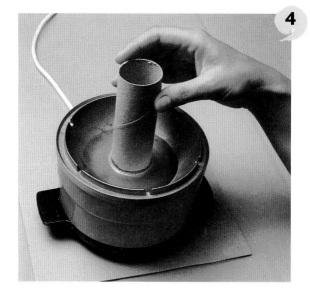

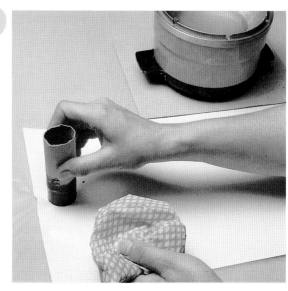

3 To get the best print from your caps, there should be a soft surface under your paper to press into. Lay a folded blanket or towel under the plastic sheet on your work surface to make a soft bed.

4 Lay a sheet of paper on top of your printing bed. Heat the wax until it has melted, and put your cap into the wax. Cardboard sometimes fizzes the first time you put it in, so don't worry. Count to 10 to allow the wax to penetrate and warm the cardboard.

5 As you lift it from the wax, gently shake off the excess wax once or twice. Hold a pad of material underneath it to catch any further drips as you take it to the paper.

6 Print the wax onto the paper by pressing the cap down firmly. If the wax stays white and opaque, it is not hot enough. The paper should turn darker and become more translucent when it comes into contact with the wax.

7 You can do more than one print before going back to the wax pot, but each successive print will leave a thinner deposit as the wax is used up and cools. Three or four impressions are usually the maximum.

8 Combine different cap prints to build up a pattern.

9

10

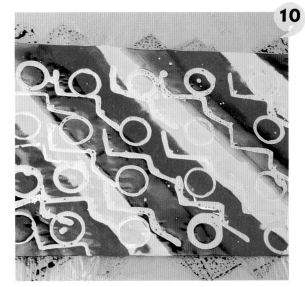

11

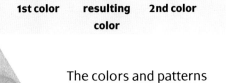

1st color	resulting color	2nd color

SAFETY FIRST

- Whichever way you use to melt the wax do not allow it to smoke – the fumes are unpleasant, unhealthy to breathe in for long periods and unnecessary, for the wax is hot enough before it smokes. A temperature of 270° is an ideal constant temperature, and you can test this with a wax thermometer.
- If the wax becomes overheated and ignites, smother the container with a fireproof lid. **Never** introduce water, which will spit and spread.
- Always work in a well-ventilated area.

9 Mix the dye using ¼ teaspoon of dye powder and 2 tablespoons soda solution for each color (see page 10). Red, yellow, and blue have been used here. You can apply the dye in stripes or paint different colors inside the various wax-surrounded shapes.

10 When the dye is dry, iron out the wax. If you do not want the "halo" shapes, cover the unwaxed areas with wax while they are still warm from ironing, which makes it quick and economical on wax, and then iron out again. All the "halos" will disappear.

11 Try mixing your dyes to see what other colors you can make.

The colors and patterns you achieve will be as varied as your imagination.

SUN CALENDAR

Working on fabric is slightly more complicated than producing batik paper, but it is not difficult and the process can still be kept simple while giving effective results. The fabric must be 100 percent natural fiber — cotton, linen, silk, for example — or viscose rayon. Any manmade fibers in the fabric, as in cotton polyester, may appear to take up the dye, only to wash out at a later rinse stage, giving disappointing results. When the dyes are mixed with an alkali (the solution of sodas), a chemical reaction takes place that allows a permanent bonding of dye and fiber — hence the name, fiber-reactive dyes. Once the chemical reaction between dye and alkali has begun, it continues for 2 to 4 hours, after which the dyestuff will no longer be fiber-reactive. As with synthetics, it may appear to take up, only to wash away later, although it can be used up on paper batiks if you can't bear to throw it away. The dye powder, however, can be stored indefinitely if it is kept in closed containers in a cool atmosphere and away from the light.

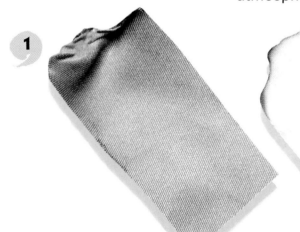

You will need
◊ Basic equipment, plus
◊ 2 squares in prepared fabric, 8 × 8in and 3 × 3in
◊ Small blanket or towel

Cap-making kit
◊ Masking tape
◊ Scissors/mat knife
◊ Empty cereal boxes
◊ Boxes
◊ Corrugated cardboard
◊ Cardboard tube

1 Burning a small sample of a fabric is a good way of testing the fiber content, and the kitchen sink is a safe place to do this. Hold a lighted match to a piece of the fabric. Synthetic threads will burn quickly and leave a hard plastic residue; natural fibers burn slowly, and leave a soft ash.

2 You will need a piece of prepared cotton about 8 inches square. Any oil or dressing in the fabric may prevent the dye from penetrating, and they must be removed by scouring. This is achieved by boiling the fabric for 5 minutes in a solution made to the proportions of 2 teaspoons detergent to 2 pints water. You can use 2 teaspoons washing soda crystals instead, but this may affect the surface of your boiling pan. Rinse the fabric in clear water, allow it to dry, and iron to a smooth finish. The fabric is now prepared and is also preshrunk.

3

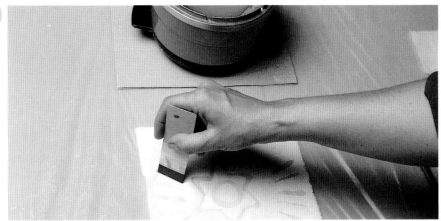

6

4

5

3 Lay the prepared fabric on a soft bed and heat the wax to approximately 270°. Have your homemade caps ready, and wax the areas you wish to remain white. If the wax is at the right temperature, you will see a change in tone of the fabric just as you did with the paper. If the wax is white and opaque, the fibers are not being penetrated by the wax and will not resist the dye.

4 Mix ¼ teaspoon yellow dye with 2 tablespoons soda solution (see page 10).

5 Apply the dye with a piece of cut sponge. Remember to wear rubber gloves.

6 Dye the test piece for experimenting with overdyeing later. Leave it to dry naturally; this will depend on the temperature of your room. You can speed up the drying time with some warm air, but if you use a hairdryer, take care not to melt the wax. Apply wax to the dried fabric in the areas you want to keep yellow. The facial detail can be added with a small brush.

7

8

9

7 Mix red dye as yellow above. Try it out on your test piece of fabric. Add more dye powder if the color is too weak or more soda solution if the color is too strong. Apply to your square and allow to dry.

8 Use a brush and cap to wax the areas you want to stay orange.

9 Mix blue dye and test it on your sample piece before applying it. When the dye has dried completely, remove the fabric from the plastic sheet and iron out the wax between sheets of newspaper.

CALENDAR

You can mount your finished piece and perhaps attach a calendar below it. You can buy ready-made window mats, or you could get the piece mounted by a framer.

DOLLY BAGS

When you apply the colors all over the fabric each time, the range of colors you can achieve is limited to the shades resulting from overdyeing. Painting on the dye in "pools" of fabric surrounded by wax, in the technique known as pool dyeing, gives tremendous possibilities for color combinations to exist side by side, and the opportunities are limited only by your dye-mixing abilities. Using the dye in this way requires the addition of urea, which is a byproduct of natural gas. In this process small amounts of dye are painted onto the fabric, rather than the fabric being immersed completely in a dye bath as in traditional batik, and urea is used to delay the drying process. This is important because fibers and dye react while the fabric is wet, and the longer this process takes, the better the dye fixing will be – so, no speeding up of the drying from now on. Urea also helps to dissolve the dye more easily and thoroughly, maximizing the color intensity. This project also involves the use of a sponge "brush," saving colors with wax, and boiling out wax.

You will need
◊ Basic equipment, plus
◊ Prepared cotton fabric, 21¾ × 16½in
◊ Lining material, 21¾ × 16½in
◊ Blanket or towel
◊ 2 wooden sticks, 6in long – old brush handles or straight twigs, for example
◊ Small paint brush (optional)
◊ Soft pencil
◊ Ruler

Cap-making kit
◊ Masking tape
◊ Cardboard tubes
◊ Corrugated paper/cereal boxes
◊ Scissors/mat knife

Making up the bags
◊ Scissors
◊ Pins
◊ Thread
◊ Sewing machine or needles if you prefer to sew by hand
◊ 1yd lacing to make the drawstring handles

1 To make up a solution, dissolve 1 teaspoon of urea with 1 pint warm water. If you are going to use it immediately, do not use water warmer than 122° because fiber-reactives are cold dyes and must not be heated above this temperature. This, like the soda solution, is usable for 10–14 days if it is kept in an airtight container.

2 Using the selective dyeing process, you can make three bags with different color schemes. The bags have a base with a diameter of 5 inches, and the sides are 5 × 15¾ inches (all seams are included in the specifications). Mark the three strips and bases on the prepared fabric with a soft pencil and lay it on a soft bed.

3

4

5

urea solution

soda solution

6

3 Make a sponge "brush." Push one of the wooden sticks into a piece of sponge and strap it firmly in place with masking tape. Trim it to a point, ready for use. The sponge will hold more wax than a normal brush, enabling you to work for longer before having to recharge it with wax. These homemade tools are also excellent for applying dye. Heat the wax and use your sponge "brush" to apply a continuous line of wax, following your pencil lines, to separate the three strips. If you do not do this, dye will spread to areas where it is not wanted.

4 Make your cap prints in each section, making sure that each shape has a continuous wax boundary. If the wax sticks to the plastic beneath the fabric, you know it has penetrated! It will also keep your work in place while you are dyeing, preventing the unwanted transfer of color.

5 Colorfastness is obtained by combining the urea solution with the soda solution in the ratio of 1 part urea to 2 parts soda. For this project add a few drops of urea solution to ¼ teaspoon of dye powder to form a paste, then add 2 teaspoons urea solution and 4 teaspoons soda solution. This will be about full strength; if you want paler colors, reduce the dye powder.

6 When all waxing and dyeing is completed and dried, remove the fabric from the plastic sheet and iron out the wax. You will probably have noticed that the fabric becomes soft while it is warm from ironing, but stiffens again as the residue of wax in the fibers cools. You may wish to retain this quality, because the residue makes the fabric water-repellent. However, if you want the fabric less stiff, more wax can be removed by boiling the fabric in water in an old saucepan for 5 minutes, then

plunging it into cold water, using wooden tongs to transfer it from pan to bowl. The wax solidifies on the surface of the cloth and can be rubbed or scraped off. This process can be repeated to remove more wax. Finally, boil in soapy water to remove all surplus dye. Allow the dye to set in the fabric for 24 hours before using this method.

Leave the saucepan of water in which you have boiled the fabric to cool, and the wax will form a skin on the surface, which can be removed, dried, and used again. You must dry wax thoroughly before reusing it; otherwise, it will spit in the wax pot, like hot grease in a skillet.

7

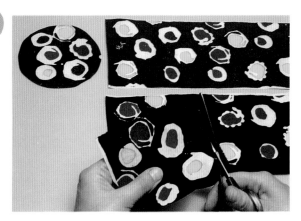

8

9

7 Once the wax has been removed to your satisfaction, cut out the fabric ready to make your bags. Allowing ¼-inch seams, sew the sides together. On each side make a buttonhole ½ inch long and running from ¾ inch to 1¼ inches from the top edge.

8 With right sides together, sew the base to the bottom edge. Turn right sides out. Cut and sew the lining material in the same way but omit the buttonholes. Leave unturned.

9 Put the lining inside the bag, turn in ¼-inch seams on both, and sew together. Sew two lines of stitching around the top of the bag, one at the top edge of the buttonholes and the other at the bottom edge to provide a channel for the drawstring. Thread through the

drawstrings, one entering and one exiting from each buttonhole.

If you want to make a larger bag, multiply the radius of the base, by 6.284 (approx 6¼) to give you the appropriate length side.

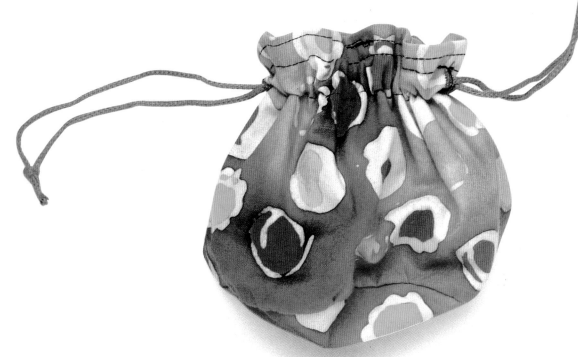

PILLOWCASE

◆

You can personalize a ready-made garment or article, as long as it is 100 percent natural fibers, by adding batik decoration of your choice. I have worked on a pillowcase here, but you can work on any article you like. However, as with all the other fabrics, it must be prepared and then laid on a soft bed that is large enough to accommodate the whole of it.

You will need
◊ Basic equipment, plus
◊ Blanket
◊ Dye brushes or sponges
◊ Prepared cotton pillowcases
◊ Caps — two sizes of cardboard tube, flat cardboard to bend into shape, and masking tape to hold small shape in position

1 When you use your found or home-made caps to apply the wax, you must bear in mind that you have two layers to penetrate. Recharge the cap with wax for each stamp, and make sure that it is hot enough by counting to five each time you put the cap into the wax pot.

2 If the wax does not penetrate properly, the underside of the completed article may be disappointing. As with the dolly bags, if the wax sticks to the plastic sheet, leave it to hold your fabric in place while you apply the dye.

3 You will need more dyestuff for this article. Use ½ teaspoon dye powder with 2 tablespoons urea solution and 4 tablespoons soda solution. If you want paler shades, reduce the amount of dye powder or increase the chemical solutions.

4 Remember to wear your gloves. Dye the lightest areas first and allow to dry. If the color has leaked at all, wax again before adding the dark background, which will cover up any unwanted dye.

5 When the design is completed and dry, remove the pillowcase from the plastic sheet and iron out the bulk of the wax. Put it in for a drycleaning cycle so that the fabric regains its original softness.

There is no need to start with a white background. Immersion dyeing, which is introduced in the next project, will allow you to start with any color you like, but you must remember that all subsequent colors will be affected by the original shade.

GARMENT FABRIC

Large pieces of fabric can be quite easily batiked. The waxing is done in stages on a soft bed, and the fabric is then immersed in dye to guarantee full penetration and evenness of color.

You will need
◊ Basic equipment, plus
◊ Blanket
◊ Plastic bucket with a minimum capacity of 1 gallon
◊ Bowl with a minimum capacity of 1 gallon
◊ Paper and fabric for experimenting with caps and dyes
◊ 2yd prepared lightweight cotton fabric

Cap-making kit
◊ Masking tape
◊ Scissors/mat knife
◊ Empty cereal boxes
◊ Corrugated cardboard
◊ Cardboard tube
◊ Empty ring from wide roll of tape

1

2

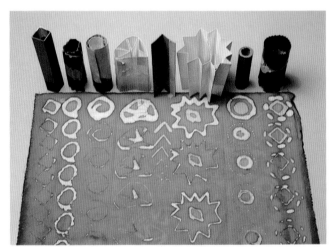

3

HINTS AND TIPS

FIXING COLORS

● Fixing is improved in a humid atmosphere. Short bursts of steam from a kettle, introduced intermittently over the 2–3 hour drying period, can provide the necessary humidity.

◐ The evenness of color can be enhanced by adding the salt in three stages in the first 15 minutes of the dyeing process. However, the fabric must be removed each time more salt is added, which makes the procedure a bit too complicated for a beginner. For this reason I have suggested that all the salt be added at the same time.

1 Make some cardboard caps and experiment on paper with them until you have a design you are happy with.

2 Try the caps on fabric to see how many prints you can get from each dip in the wax and how they change as the wax cools and runs out.

3 Make as large a soft bed as your blanket and work surface will allow. Lay down the first section of your fabric, and arrange a chair on each side to hold it off the floor while you are waxing. Lift the fabric at intervals as you work to prevent it from sticking to the plastic when you want to move on to the next section.

4

5

> **CALCULATING THE DYE BATH INGREDIENTS**
>
> Multiply the dry weight of fabric before waxing by 20 — 6 ounces × 20 = 120 ounces = 7½ pints. For every 2 pints of dye bath you need:
> - ½—2 teaspoons dye powder
> - 2 tablespoons salt
> - 2 teaspoons soda ash or 4 teaspoons soda crystals

4 When the first waxing is complete, prepare the dye bath. These ingredients are enough for about 6 ounces dry weight of fabric, which is about what 2 yards of cotton fabric should weigh. Dissolve 6 tablespoons salt in 3 ounces warm water and set aside. Dissolve 6 teaspoons soda ash (or 12 teaspoons soda crystals) in 3 ounces warm water and set aside.

5 Make a paste of 1½—6 teaspoons yellow dye powder in warm water. Do not use water warmer than 122°. Add some more water so that it will pour easily.

6 Add 7½ pints water to the dye and stir. Add the dissolved salt and stir. Salt is added to this dye recipe to facilitate penetration, to promote an even quality of dyeing, and to get the best color from the dye powder.

7 Immerse the waxed fabric and test piece in clean, cold water and shake off the excess.

8 Transfer the fabric to the dye bath. Immerse it completely, agitating it to guarantee good penetration of the dye.

9 Remove it after 15 minutes and put it in a bowl.

10 Add the dissolved soda to the dye bath, then return and immerse the fabric for a further 45 minutes, stirring occasionally. Remove the fabric, rinse in cold water until the water runs clear, then hang to drip dry. This is part of the fixing process.

6

7

8

9

10

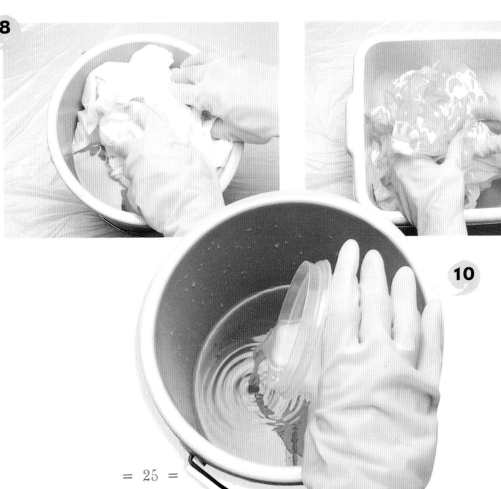

11 When the fabric is completely dry, return it to the soft bed and do the second waxing. This time wax everything you want to stay yellow.

12 Follow the same recipe and procedure as before, but using blue dye powder instead of yellow. Test the color on your sample piece first.

13 As the fabric moves around in the dye bath, some of the wax will be bent and crack, and dye will be able to penetrate the fibers. This is what gives batik its traditional crackle effect. Wax cracks more readily and cleanly when it is cold, and this is why the fabric is soaked in cold water before it is immersed in the dye bath. The cracking is further controlled by crushing the fabric to a greater or lesser extent before and while it is being dyed.

It is easier to boil out the bulk of the wax from a large piece of fabric than to iron it. Dry-clean it to restore the original softness, and then it will be ready to make into the article of your choice. If you machine wash the article at home afterward do so on a cool wash – 104° – and wash separately for the first few washes, especially if you have used intense colors.

PILLOW COVER

◆

As we have seen, it was the Javanese who invented the canting. Although it is not easy to use, once you have mastered the techniques you will find that the canting will provide a continuous flow of hot wax that will allow you to do fine line or dot work that would not otherwise be possible. There are many different shapes of these metal wax reservoirs available, but they all have one or more spouts through which the wax flows. The diameter of the spouts is one of the factors dictating the width of a line or the size of a dot of the wax applied to the fabric; speed, heat, and angle of use are others.

Wax can be most easily applied to fine cottons and silks because the wax can penetrate more quickly than on thicker or more coarsely woven fabrics like linen. You will draw a more confident, freer, and finer line if the tool can move smoothly and easily across the surface. If you go more slowly to allow wax to penetrate a thicker fabric, you will be more likely to produce wobbly, more uneven, and thicker lines. The heat of the wax also affects the speed with which it flows through the spout and how much it spreads in the fabric, and this is particularly evident when you are working on fine fabrics, such as silk. Remember that the same spout will produce lines of different widths on different fabrics and with the wax at different temperatures.

You will need
◊ Basic equipment, plus
◊ Soft pencil
◊ Wooden frame
◊ Thumbtacks
◊ Prepared cotton fabric, 17 × 17in

1 An abstract design, which will give you maximum freedom to experiment with the cantings, is suggested for a pillow cover. Lay the prepared piece of fabric on your work surface and use a soft pencil to mark the diagonal and horizontal crosses lightly as a guide to keep the design symmetrical.

2 At first, you will find that canting work is easiest on stretched fabric. You can use an old picture frame, if it is firmly jointed and not warped. Tack the center of each side and then the corners. The fabric needs to be taut, but take care that you do not pull the weave out of alignment, or the image will be distorted when you take the fabric from the frame.

3

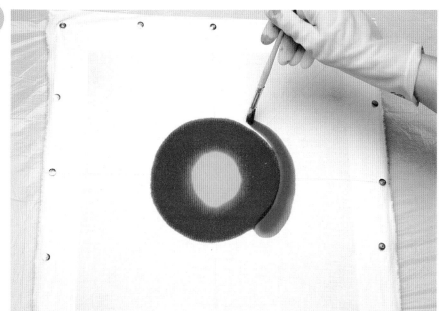

4

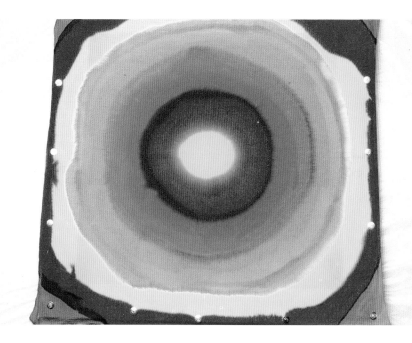

5

3 Before you begin waxing, mix the dyes – 6 tablespoons of each should be plenty. I have used red, yellow, and turquoise (see page 22). Apply the dyes to the fabric, allowing them to mingle with each other at the edges to create a colorful, softly diffused effect.

4 Keep the colors light and bright. Allow the fabric to dry completely.

5 Heat the wax and put the canting in it for at least 30 seconds so that the metal bowl can warm up and help to keep the wax hot. Fill the reservoir about half full so that wax does not flow over the top while you are working. Use a piece of soft, absorbent cloth to remove excess wax and to catch any drips as you carry the canting from the wax pot to the fabric.

6

7

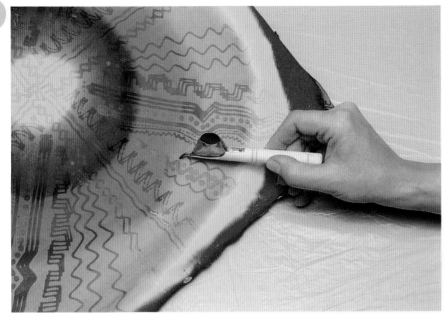

6 Rest your frame at an angle and also hold the canting at an angle as you work. The angle affects the flow of wax from the spout, and you will have to experiment to get the flow you want, but do not hold it at such a sharp angle that wax flows out of the back onto your fingers!

7 When waxing is complete, mix 3 ounces of black dyestuff using ½ teaspoon dye powder and apply it over the fabric with a sponge. Remember to have the sheet of plastic underneath to catch any drips and to wear rubber gloves to protect your fingers. Fiber-reactive dyes increase in intensity when they are overdyed, and this is particularly true with black, which looks darker and richer when it is applied twice, as was done here to cover the underlying bright dyes. When the fabric is completely dry, iron out and dry clean it before making the pillow cover.

FISH ON SILK

◇

Silk is a much more delicate fabric than cotton, and it requires a different treatment and a different technique. It has to be prepared for the same reasons as cotton, but it should never be boiled. A rinse in warm water containing detergent is sufficient. The wax can be cooler because the weave is so fine, and you can use a canting with a smaller spout because the wax will penetrate the fabric easily. The dyes will look less intense than on cotton and linen, and they will also react differently.

You will need
◊ Basic equipment, plus
◊ Prepared silk, 6 × 6in
◊ Sheet of acetate, 8 × 10in
◊ Cardboard frame with an image area 5¼ × 5¼in
◊ Masking tape
◊ Mixing palette
◊ Small, soft dyebrush – watercolor brush size no. 4

1

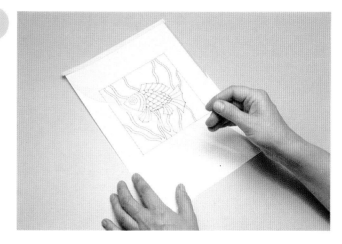

1 Keep to quite a simple image to begin with. You can use the fish shown here or draw an image of your own. Because silk is so fine, you will be able to see through it and use it like tracing paper to do your waxing. Put a layer of acetate between the image and your silk to prevent the wax from picking up any ink, which might transfer to the silk when you are ironing out the wax.

2

3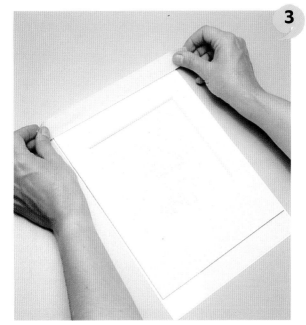

4

5

6

7

2 You can use a cardboard frame on which to stretch the silk. Although you can use corrugated cardboard, the best kind is heavy mat board or the card used for sales displays. If you use the fish, the cutout window needs to be 5¼ × 5¼ inches. Tape the prepared fabric to the frame so that it is taut but not distorted. Position the stretched fabric over the image.

3 Tape it securely at the top, but just catch the sides and bottom with small pieces of tape so that you can separate the layers to check your progress.

4 Working with the fabric and canting at an angle, draw a line of wax around the perimeter of the image area, using the edge of the frame to guide the canting. This line will prevent the dye from spreading into your cardboard frame.

5 Following the lines of the image underneath, wax around the different "pools" of color that you want. Make sure there are no gaps in the lines themselves or at the points where they join. This prevents dye from spreading to unwanted areas.

6 You will need very small amounts of dye for the fish. Mix a solution of 1 teaspoon urea solution and 2 teaspoons of soda solution and use them to mix the colors you want. Use a palette and treat the dye powder as if it were powder paint, mixing it with the chemicals solutions as if they were water.

7 Test the colors on a sample.

8

9

10

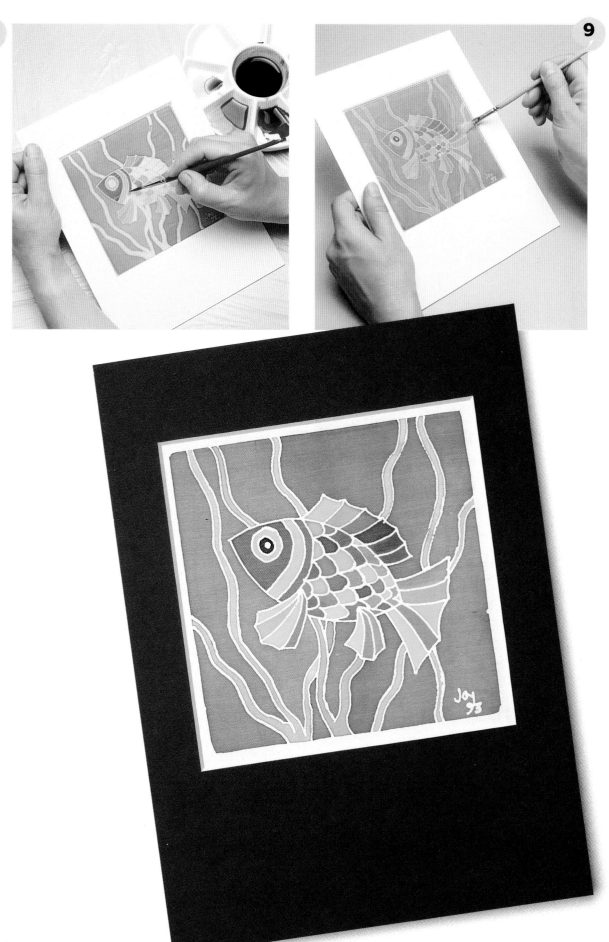

8 Remove your stretched fabric from the acetate-covered image and paint on the dyes.

9 When the dye is completely dry, which happens much more quickly on silk than on cotton, wax the whole area before ironing out to prevent "halos" from forming.

10 Be very careful when you iron out silk. Creases that form at this stage are very difficult to remove. It is better to use blank newsprint, and do not pick up your ironed piece until it has cooled completely or it will be distorted when the wax cools. Ironing flat again can sometimes be difficult.

You could position your finished batik between two layers of plexiglass and hang it against a window or mount it on a white backing sheet and frame it. Spray adhesive is an efficient and easy way of mounting silk on paper.

WINDOW SHADE

◦───◇───◦

When cotton batik is held against the light, the effect is similar to that of stained glass windows. The dyes are seen at their very best, with the light giving extra vibrancy to all the colors. A window shade is, therefore, a good way of displaying your batik expertise. Choose a small window for your first attempt. This project will cover an area 26 inches wide and 44 inches long.

The materials allow ½ inch hems at the side edges and 4 inches at the top and bottom for attaching to the shade kit. The fabric may shrink when it is boiled, so cut the material at least 1 inch larger all around than the measurements given for the prepared fabric.

You will need
◊ Basic equipment, plus
◊ Prepared fabric, 27 × 52in
◊ Wooden frame, 27 × 27in
◊ Thumbtacks
◊ Tapemeasure
◊ Long ruler or straightedge
◊ Masking tape
◊ Soft pencil

Plan of window shade

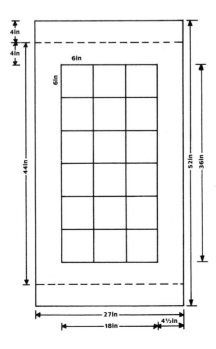

1

2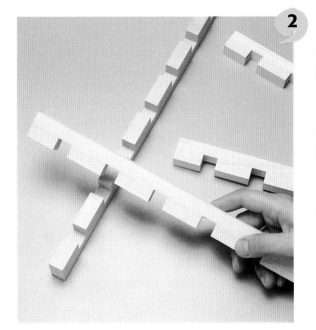

3

4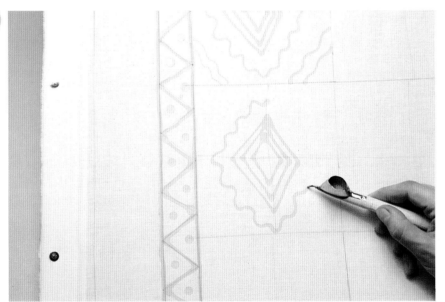

5

1 Lay the fabric on a firm surface and use a soft pencil to mark off 4 inches at top and bottom. Draw a margin of a further 4 inches inside these lines and on each side a margin of 4½ inches. The inside area is 18 inches by 36 inches, so the repeat motif has been made 6 inches square to fit three times across and six times down. Mark these squares. The border pattern needs only a ruler's width line marked in to keep the width of the snake line constant, with the points 1 inch along the edges.

2 A frame about 27 inches square would be ideal for stretching your fabric so that it can be worked in two manageable sections. These adjustable frames, which slot together, are available from craft stores in a range of sizes, or you could use an old picture frame.

3 Wax in the border pattern. When the first section is complete, move the fabric up the frame and position the second half. Move it carefully so that you do not crack the wax lines; otherwise, the colors will seep where you do not want them to.

4 The only extra guides you might need are the vertical and horizontal crosses so that you can place the points of the diamond shapes in each square. Let your canting run freely and enjoy applying the undulating lines. They will all look similar enough to work well visually, but different enough to add interest.

5 It is easier to apply dye if the fabric is in a complete length. If it is laid on a plastic sheet, the dye may collect and cross over the wax lines. Laying it on an absorbent surface, such as newspaper, can make this less likely, but tends to suck the dye away from the fabric. If

6

7

8

you can suspend the material in some way, there will be fewer color accidents and the finished design will look more the way you intended. You can suspend the fabric from a shelf or door frame, which is how I applied the smaller areas of color here. Remember to work from light to dark with your dyes and to wax them as they dry to prevent any accidents with darker colors later.

6 The final background was applied with a sponge while the fabric was suspended between two lengths of 2-inch-square wood resting on the work surface.

7 It is better to work horizontally when larger areas are being dyed because the fabric will hold the dye, which will not drain away to the base, as happens when hanging vertically, resulting in some color loss at the top.

8 When all the dye is completely dried, wax all over to avoid "halos," remembering to lift the fabric between applications of wax. Iron out and either leave the fabric stiff and waterproof, or get it dry-cleaned after ironing and spray it with fabric protector and water repellant so that the shade can be wiped clean. Your batik fabric is ready to turn into a shade that will bring the beauty of stained glass to your window.

PORTRAITS

◆

The techniques you used to make the Sun Calendar — successive waxing and dyeing to build up the image — can be used to reproduce photographs. This time, instead of using caps on cotton, you will wax with a canting onto silk. Silk is used because of its transparency, which allows you to see the image easily through the fabric. Choose an image with quite a lot of contrast — it could be your partner, child, pet, or even the car! It doesn't matter if it is black and white or color.

You will need
◊ Basic equipment, plus
◊ Image — photograph or picture from a magazine, for example
◊ Enlarged photostat of the chosen image
◊ Acetate
◊ Prepared silk, 11in wider all around than projected finished image
◊ Cardboard frame with inside dimensions of projected finished image
◊ Blank newsprint

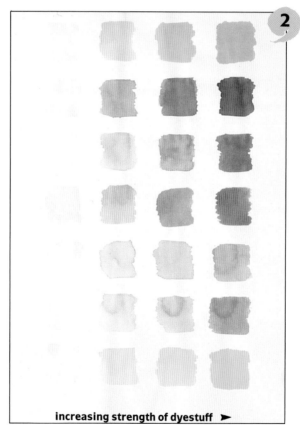

increasing strength of dyestuff ►

1 Enlarge the image on a photocopier. As a guide, increase the face to measure at least 6 inches from crown to chin. Cover the image with acetate.

2 Plan to have three shades in addition to white. These do not have to be grays — you might like to work in shades of one color by mixing different strengths of dyestuff.

3 Prepare and attach your silk to the cardboard frame (see page 31). Tape the image in position behind the stretched silk and draw the line of wax around the image area (see page 31). Wax in the areas to be kept white using a brush or sponge for large areas and soften the edges by applying the wax as dots with the canting.

4

5

6

7

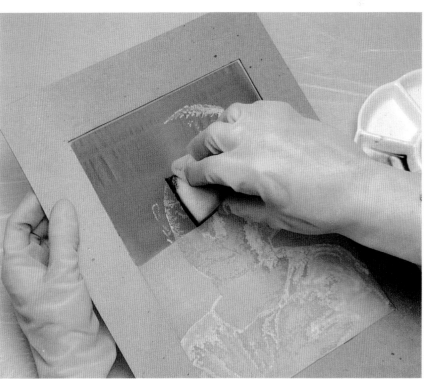

4 Remove the silk from the image ready to dye the first shade. Mix the lightest dye (shade 1) and apply it with a piece of sponge. Do not overload the sponge with liquid or the wax outline to your image will be unable to contain the dye. Remember to wear rubber gloves.

5 Use the dotting technique to wax the areas to be saved as shade 1.

6 Mix the next dye (shade 2) and test on the reverse side of the picture.

7 Apply shade 2 with a soft sponge.

8

9

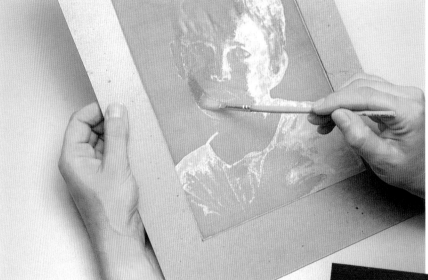

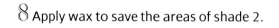

8 Apply wax to save the areas of shade 2.

9 Mix the last and darkest dye, shade 3, and apply as before. When it is completely dry, wax the remaining areas to avoid "halos" from forming after ironing out.

Iron out the wax, leaving the silk to lie flat until it is cool. Mount for display.

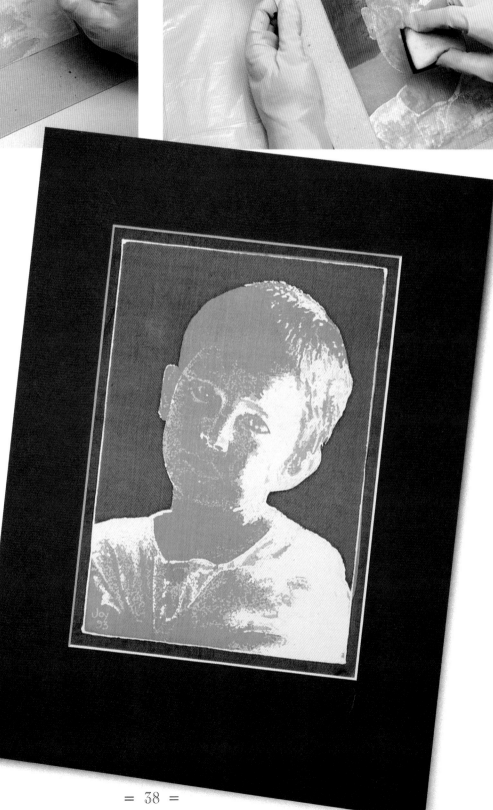

DECORATED EGGS

—◇—

Now it is time to try something completely different. You have worked with cantings on cotton and silk, but now you can experiment on a hard, curved surface. Simple designs can look extremely effective, and a few differently colored eggs can look very attractive together in a bowl.

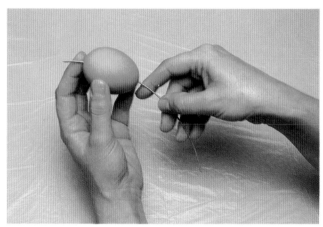

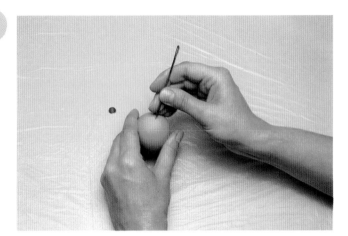

1

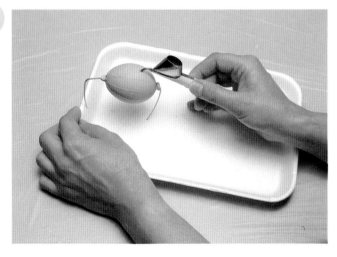

3

You will need
◊ Basic equipment, plus
◊ Eggs
◊ Thumbtack and long needle
◊ Fine wire
◊ Low-tack adhesive plastic or modeling clay
◊ Styrofoam block
◊ General-purpose plastic wood
◊ Spray varnish

1 Blow an egg by piercing a hole at each end with a thumbtack. Enlarge the holes carefully by chipping away tiny fragments at a time with a needle. Blow the contents into a container so that you can have scrambled eggs later.

2 Thread fine wire through the holes, keeping the egg in place on the wire with adhesive plastic or modeling clay.

3 Bend the wire at each end of the egg and push the ends into a styrofoam block or tray to stabilize the egg while you are working on it. Heat the canting. Try simple patterns to start with.

4 Paint on the dye with a brush. Mix the colors to full strength in the same way as for fabric.

5

6

7

8

9

5 When the dye is completely dry, you can do a second waxing.

6 Paint on the second color.

7 Remove the wax by holding the eggs by the wire over a gentle heat for a few seconds, turning it all the time. You should hold the wire in an insulating cloth so that you do not burn your fingers. A safer way is to warm the egg in an oven on a low temperature, 250°, for 2–3 minutes. Use a soft, absorbent cloth to rub off the melted wax. Return it to the heat for a few moments if any wax remains unmelted.

8 So that you can handle the egg without dye coming off on your fingers, spray the finished egg with varnish. Make an improvised spraying booth with an old file or cardboard box cut open as a back shield, and support the egg on an upside-down foil dish.

9 Remove the wire when the varnish is dry. Seal the holes in the ends of the egg with a small amount of filler either colored with dye to match the rest of the egg, or painted after application. Spray a little varnish over each end when the filler has dried.

OWL PICTURE

In all the other projects in this book, you have used wax as a resist so that you could selectively dye areas of paper or fabric. Another use for this resist is to "undye" areas of an image. By using ordinary household bleach on fabric that is already dyed a strong color, you can "discharge" the dye — that is, remove the dye already in the fabric.

Varying the dilution strength of the bleach and/or the length of time it is in contact with the fabric allows you to create an image in varying shades of the original color. The strength of the bleach solutions and contact times given here are only approximate, and you will have to experiment on the particular fabric you are using because dyes react in different ways.

You will need
◊ Basic equipment, plus
◊ Prepared, pre-dyed cotton fabric
  11 × 11in
◊ Household bleach
◊ Wooden frame
◊ Thumbtacks
◊ Plastic tray larger than the fabric
◊ Sodium metabisulfite
◊ Masking tape
◊ Soft pencil

SAFETY FIRST

● **If any bleach gets onto your skin or into your eyes, rinse immediately with plenty of cold, clean water.**

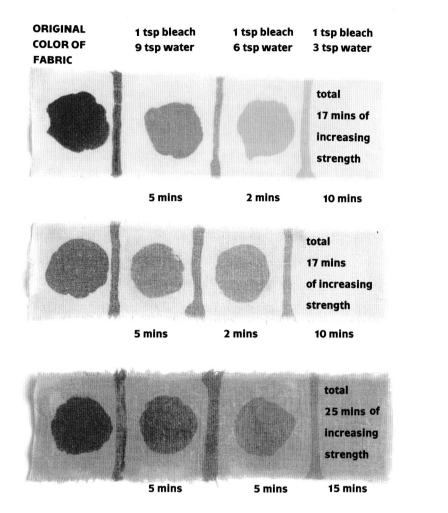

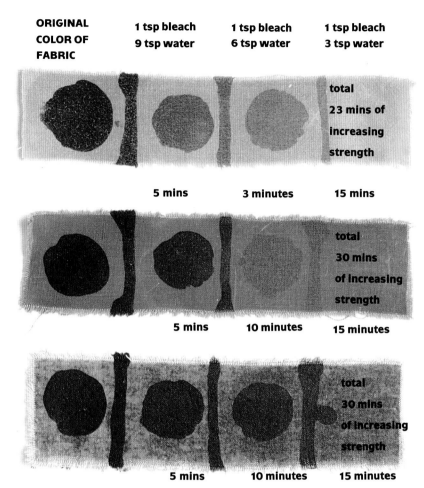

ORIGINAL COLOR OF FABRIC	1 tsp bleach 9 tsp water	1 tsp bleach 6 tsp water	1 tsp bleach 3 tsp water
			total 17 mins of increasing strength
	5 mins	2 mins	10 mins
			total 17 mins of increasing strength
	5 mins	2 mins	10 mins
			total 25 mins of increasing strength
	5 mins	5 mins	15 mins

ORIGINAL COLOR OF FABRIC	1 tsp bleach 9 tsp water	1 tsp bleach 6 tsp water	1 tsp bleach 3 tsp water
			total 23 mins of increasing strength
	5 mins	3 minutes	15 mins
			total 30 mins of increasing strength
	5 mins	10 minutes	15 minutes
			total 30 mins of increasing strength
	5 mins	10 minutes	15 minutes

1 Some dyes discharge more readily than others, so always do a test on a small piece of your fabric before you start your main work. Never use neat bleach — it will rot the fibers — and never use bleach on silk — it will rot the fabric completely. The strongest solution you should use is 1 part bleach to 3 parts water. It is better to extend the time than to increase the strength of the bleach.

2 Black dyes discharge to very different colors according to the bias of color in the make-up of the dye.

3 Transfer your image to the fabric using a light box or using masking tape to keep everything in place against a window. Until you are confident enough to draw freehand, it might be sensible to avoid black fabric, because it is harder to see through. If pencil does not show up on your fabric, use white chalk or pastel crayon.

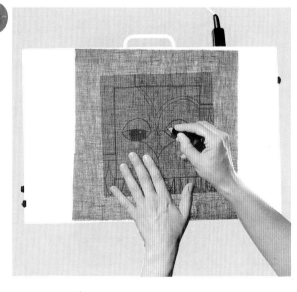

4 Pin your prepared fabric to the frame, and use cantings or brushes to wax the areas or lines that are to be the darkest shade.

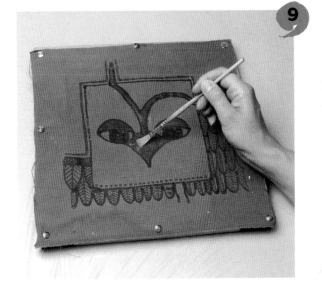

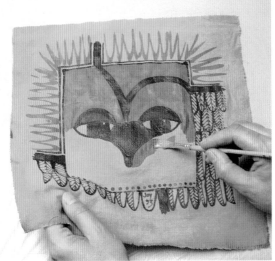

5 Prepare the neutralizing solution in readiness for step 8 later. Dissolve ½ teaspoon of sodium metabisulfite to 2 pints of water, which should be at a temperature of 105°. You will find sodium metabisulfite in the home-brewing section, where it is sold for sterilizing equipment.

6 Mix a weak bleach solution of 1 teaspoon bleach to 3 tablespoons water and apply it with a sponge or cotton balls. Protect your hands with rubber gloves.

7 When enough dye has discharged, which should take 5–10 minutes, rinse the fabric in cold water.

8 Transfer the fabric to the sodium metabisulfite solution and leave for 15 minutes. This will neutralize the bleach and prevent it from damaging the fibers. Rinse again in cold water.

9 Remount the fabric on the frame and when it is completely dry, wax the areas you want to keep the same shade as that achieved by the first bleaching/discharging.

10 Mix a stronger bleach solution of 1 teaspoon bleach to 2 tablespoons water, and apply as before. After 5–10 minutes rinse in cold water, transfer to a fresh solution of sodium metabisulfite, which must be renewed each time it is used. Remount the fabric on the frame for the last waxing to save the last shade before the final bleaching.

11 This time, mix a strong bleach solution of 1 teaspoon bleach to 1 tablespoon water.

12 When all the dye has been removed, rinse and neutralize as before.

13 When it is completely dry, iron out the wax. Mount and frame.

WALL HANGING

———— ◇ ————

Bleach can also be used to increase the possible range of colors when you are working on images that you do not want to be outlined by a white wax line. When you do successive immersions in dye, some colors are lost — for example, if the first color is yellow, subsequent dyeing with blue will create green; if the first color is red, subsequent dyeing with blue will create purple, and in neither case will any of the fabric be blue. In this project, which uses red and blue dye, the discharge process is used to regain the blue.

You will need
◊ Basic equipment, plus
◊ Prepared cotton fabric, 24 × 36in
◊ Soft pencil
◊ Old blanket
◊ Plastic bucket with a minimum capacity of 1 gallon
◊ Bowl with a minimum capacity of 1 gallon
◊ Cork
◊ Cardboard tube
◊ Plastic tray
◊ Bleach
◊ Sodium metabisulfite
◊ 2 pieces of ½in doweling, each 2ft long

To finish
◊ Scissors
◊ Pins
◊ Thread
◊ Sewing machine or needles

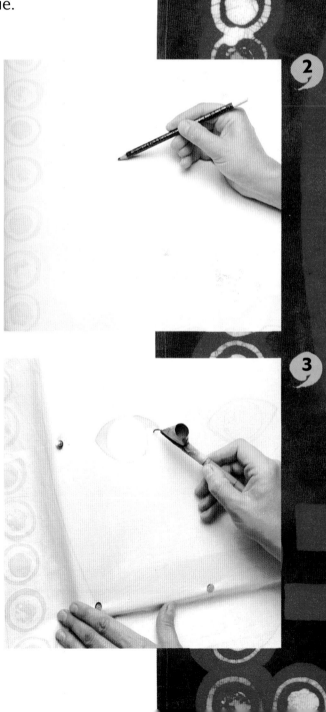

1 On the prepared fabric, use a soft pencil to mark margins of 2½ inches at the top and bottom to form the channels for the rods to fit in, and a 1-in margin on each side for a hem. These lines will act as guidelines for waxing. Lay the fabric on a soft bed and wax the white border pattern with cork and cardboard tube caps.

2 Draw an oval in the center. It does not have to be perfect, and an uneven shape will be more interesting.

3 Position the eyes about halfway up the "face." Support this area over a frame so that you can hold the fabric at an angle to wax in the white part of the eyes.

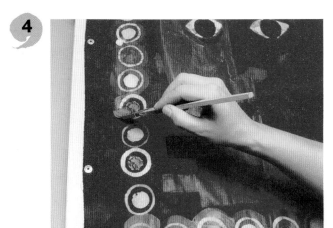

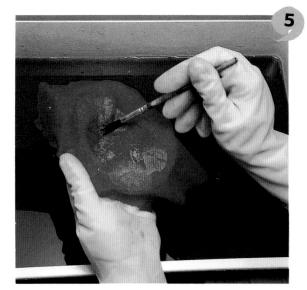

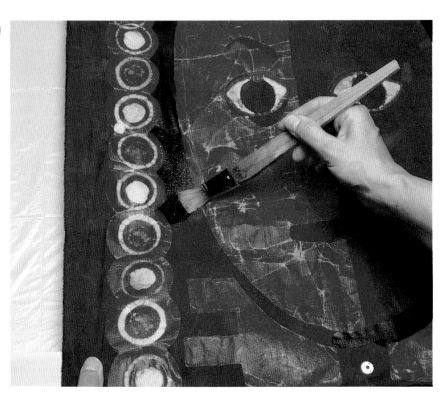

4 Prepare a red dye bath. Remember to dye a test piece to try out overdyeing colors and discharge strengths and times. Complete the border, using a brush to wax areas to stay red. Use a sponge "brush" to wax in the side of the mask face that is to stay red. This will allow you to apply the wax quickly, making it easier to draw the curved lines.

5 Prepare a blue dye bath and test the color on your sample. Adjust as necessary.

6 If you want to avoid too much crackle on the face, use a tray to hold the dye because it will be easier to keep the fabric flat.

7 When the fabric is rinsed and completely dry, return it to the work surface and wax the areas that are going to stay purple. To keep wax from sticking to the plastic sheet, lift the material as you wax. You may find it easier to mount the fabric on a frame.

8 Mix a medium-strength solution of bleach, preparing enough to cover the unwaxed areas and using proportions of 1 tablespoon bleach to 6 tablespoons water. Test on your sample piece to check the timing. You will find that the red dye discharges completely before the blue, so as soon as all the red is gone, you can rinse out the bleach solution. Neutralize and rinse.

9

10

9 If you want to intensify the blue dye, apply it as in pool batik. When it is completely dry, wax over to prevent "halos" from forming after ironing out.

10 If you want to iron out so that the fabric retains a residue of wax for waterproofing, work on a surface that is large enough to accommodate the whole piece so that it will cool flat. Otherwise, such a large piece may distort like silk.

Turn in and sew the sides. Turn over wide hems at the top and bottom to take the wooden doweling by which the finished piece will hang. The bottom rod will weight the work, making it hang better. If you prefer a softer finish, have the work dry-cleaned, then spray it with a fabric protector.

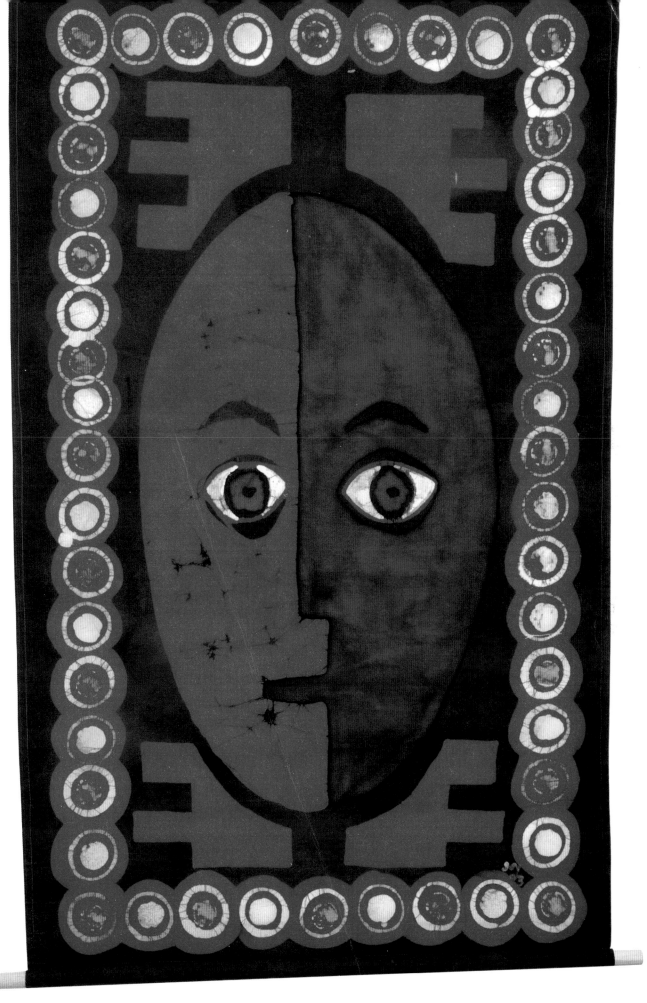

Sun Calendar page 16

Pillow Cover page 27

Owl Picture page 41

Portraits page 36

Here are some inspirational ideas to take you
further with your newly acquired skills. Each piece refers
you back to the project that uses similar techniques.

Wall Hanging page 45